Original title:
By the Coral Reefs

Copyright © 2025 Creative Arts Management OÜ
All rights reserved.

Author: Benjamin Caldwell
ISBN HARDBACK: 978-1-80581-704-8
ISBN PAPERBACK: 978-1-80581-231-9
ISBN EBOOK: 978-1-80581-704-8

Reverie in Aqua Hues

Fish in tuxedos waltz with glee,
Dancing 'round the anemone.
A crab snaps selfies, what a sight,
While seaweed sways, oh what a night!

Octopus juggles shells with flair,
Laughing at a turtle's hair.
Bubbles rise, they tickle my nose,
Who knew the ocean was so close?

Nature's Labyrinth Underwater

An eel in glasses reads a book,
While starfish pose, just take a look!
A clownfish tells a cheesy joke,
Laughter ripples, that's no hoax!

Under rocks, a hermit sighs,
Wishing for a bigger prize.
But with a shell, he makes a home,
While sea cucumbers start to roam.

Journeys Through Liquid Meadows

In a kayak, dolphins play,
Splashing water, what a ray!
A seahorse in a racing car,
Zooms around with quite the star.

Giant clams throw a banquet feast,
Where sea snails dance, to say the least.
Jellyfish float with grace and ease,
Tickling fishies like a breeze!

Twilight in the Depths

When the sun dips low, oh what a scene,
Pufferfish wearing shades, just keen.
The squids throw colors, a light show grand,
While the shrimp pass out snacks, isn't that planned?

The deep blue blushes, full of cheer,
As guests from the deep gather near.
With laughter echoing in the swell,
Life under waves is simply swell!

Derivation of the Blues

The fish, they gossip, swim in style,
With tiny glasses, oh so vile.
A crab with a hat struts on the sand,
Claiming the seas, he's in demand.

The octopus juggles shells with glee,
Dancing for shrimp, a sight to see.
The clownfish chuckles, full of cheer,
Knows he's the king, let all draw near.

Ethereal Life in Aqua Realms

A seahorse prances, tail held high,
Winks at a starfish, oh me, oh my!
With bubbles floating, they make a tune,
A concert of laughter beneath the moon.

The jellyfish glides, a squishy ghost,
While fishy friends share popcorn, a toast!
They giggle and wiggle, what a sight,
Dancing together, pure delight.

Tales from the Plankton

Tiny critters with grand dreams,
Plotting their schemes with laughter and beams.
One dreams of fame on a blogger's site,
While others just argue who's taking the bite.

A krill named Phil thinks he's the star,
Wants to be famous, but no one's near!
He dances in currents, a sight to behold,
Yet still ends up in dinner for fold.

The Horizon Underneath

Beneath the waves where secrets swell,
There's a clam that sings, oh what a yell!
With pearls for notes, he holds the crowd,
His underwater concert, lively and loud.

The parrotfish munches on coral fare,
While turtles race in a slow-motion dare.
A manta ray glides with a cheeky grin,
In this aquatic circus, let the fun begin!

Lenticular Ziggurats of Coral

Beneath the waves so bright and clear,
The fish trade gossip, oh so near.
A crab with shades takes quite the stand,
Declaring himself king of the sand.

The starfish dance, forget their plight,
While sea turtles giggle, what a sight!
With every splash, a chuckle flows,
As bubbles rise in merry throes.

As the Sea Breathes

The ocean sighs, then lets out a burp,
As dolphins flip and do a little jerk.
A seaweed party starts with a sway,
While clownfish laugh and swim away.

The jellyfish float, all slippery and bright,
Their graceful moves cause fish to take flight.
A tangle of laughter, a burst of delight,
As waves tickle shores with all of their might.

Geysers of Color Underwater

Colors explode like a surprise confetti,
A parrotfish grins, looking quite petty.
The corals giggle, in bright turquoise hue,
As sea urchins chuckle, saying, 'Who knew?'

Anemones wave, a comical kite,
They dance and they jiggle with all of their might.
Stingrays glide by, with a wink and a glide,
In this underwater carnival, there's laughter inside.

Reflection in a Wave's Heart

Waves crash and giggle, reflecting pure glee,
A seagull squawks at a crab in the spree.
The fish wear hats, a flair for the fun,
With seaweed boas, they prance and they run.

Mirrored mischief in drops of the sea,
A clam tells tales, 'Come gather with me!'
The tide holds secrets beneath its warm breath,
While the ocean laughs, teasing life and death.

The Floating Gardens of Atlantis

In gardens grand beneath the sea,
The fish wear hats, as strange as can be,
Seahorses do a tango dance,
While octopuses steal your glance.

A crab with shades is sipping lime,
He claims it's party time, sublime!
Nemo's cousins throw a bash,
With bubbles, giggles, and a splash.

Turtles with their neon shells,
Have tales of treasure they like to tell,
They spin and twirl in pure delight,
Under disco balls, oh what a sight!

So dive on in, don't be late,
Where every fish is up to date,
In goofy glee, they dance around,
In the floating gardens, joy is found.

Treasure Troves of Marine Life

Underwater banks with treasure chests,
Where fish play poker, taking bets,
Clams clap hands and sing a tune,
As dolphins juggle with a moon.

Octopuses wear pirate hats,
Claiming crowns and tips of spats,
Their treasure maps are quite absurd,
Leading to snacks, not gold, don't be cured!

A starfish king gives royal terms,
To lazy worms with funny squirms,
"Finders keepers," they all shout,
While sea turtles swim about.

Join the fun, don your gear,
There's laughter flowing everywhere,
In the troves of gooey delight,
Where every fish is out of sight!

Echoes of Ancient Sea Bed

Down where the echoes softly play,
A whale sings loudly, come what may,
With tuneful notes and rhythmic sways,
Seashells nod their heads in praise.

The ancient rocks have stories shared,
Of jellybeans and fish that dared,
To dance with sharks in shaggy crates,
While clownfish giggle, oh the fates!

Turtles whisper to the deep,
"Let's throw a party, count the sheep,"
As seagrass sways in joyful tunes,
And crabby dancers shake like loons.

In echoes where the sea meets sky,
The fish all laugh, they leap and fly,
With joyful splashes all around,
In ancient beds, pure joy is found.

Secrets Entwined in Seaweed

Amidst the seaweed, secrets slip,
Where sneaky snails take a bubble trip,
They whisper tales of sunken ships,
With funny faces, and dainty quips.

A lobster joins their silliness,
In bright disguise, a wig no less,
He jokes about his crabby friend,
Who lost his keys, oh what a trend!

They giggle at the fishes' flair,
Who swim with wigs and a bit of hair,
In bubbles of laughter, they cavort,
Creating joy, a merry sport.

So dive into this leafy maze,
Where giggles echo in playful ways,
Among the secrets tangled tight,
In seaweed's grip, all feels just right.

Beneath the Waves

In waters deep where fish do play,
A clownfish cracks jokes all day.
He tells a tale of wobbly legs,
While starfish giggle, clutching their pegs.

An octopus juggles, sneaky and sly,
With fancy moves, oh me, oh my!
Seahorses dance in a waltz so bright,
Strutting their stuff, a comical sight.

A Hidden World

Beneath the ripples, secrets unfold,
With shrimp in sunglasses, feeling so bold.
A turtle yawns, but hey, what's the fuss?
"Shell we dance?" he smirks, covering his rust.

Corals chat gossip, quite a sly bunch,
As grumpy old crabs grumble and crunch.
But in this realm, laughter's the norm,
Where each little critter brings their own charm.

A Palette of Salty Wonders

The guppies wear hats, all sizes and hues,
While jellyfish float in their quirky shoes.
"Do you see my glow?" a lanternfish beams,
"Just wait, my friends, I'm shattering dreams!"

Clams snap their shells, making wild tunes,
As trumpetfish practice their brassy cartoons.
A parrotfish cackles, with colors so bright,
Creating a ruckus, oh what a sight!

The Living Tapestry of the Ocean

A mermaid sips juice made from kelp,
While fish pals argue, can't find themselves.
"Did you take my shell?" the flatfish cries,
As eels sneak about, trying to disguise.

The sea urchins chuckle, poking their friends,
"Watch yourself, mate, it's a pointy ends!"
Rich colors swirl, in a bubbly brew,
No drama, just laughs in the deep ocean blue.

Shadows and Sunlight Beneath the Surface

Bubbles pop wildly; a game of hide and seek,
While sea turtles roll, playing hideaway peek.
"Catch me if you can!" giggles a bright fish,
As snails take their time, fulfilling their wish.

The sun dances down like glittering rays,
Tickling the fins in light-hearted plays.
Under the waves, mischief is rife,
In this funny realm, oh what a life!

The Breach Between Worlds

In a world where fish wear hats,
And dolphins laugh at jellyfats,
A whale once tried to sky-dive,
Splashing down with a belly high-five.

The octopus wore a polka-dot dress,
While turtles move with such finesse,
A crab danced sideways with a grin,
Chasing bubbles, the ultimate win.

Beneath the waves, the laughter flows,
Where seahorses wear silly bows,
Anemones giggle, they wiggle just right,
As playful fish play tag at night.

So raise a glass of seaweed tea,
To the quirkiest life, wild and free,
In a realm where laughter finds its way,
And every splash makes a perfect day.

Colors That Dance with the Current

Corals wearing vibrant hues,
They host a party with fancy shoes,
With starfish twirling, oh what a sight,
Underwater raves, bursting with light.

A clownfish juggles with a smile,
Pulls off stunts with such great style,
While shrimps breakdance on the sand,
These wild performances, oh so grand!

Rainbow parrotfish croon a tune,
As sea turtles join in, under the moon,
They sway and groove with such delight,
Dancing to bubbles, all through the night.

So if you're ever feeling low,
Join in the swim, let your joy flow,
For in this sea, we laugh and prance,
Where colors swirl in a jolly dance.

Tales from the Blue Abyss

In the depths of the blue, tales abound,
Of fish who chase their hats around,
A clam who thinks he's quite the star,
While lurking eels just laugh from afar.

The angler fish with a glowing lamp,
Tells ghost stories that make others stamp,
While lanternfish light the spooky spree,
They giggle in shadows, quite merrily.

A pufferfish, puffed up with pride,
Claims he's the strongest fish in the tide,
But every time he tries to show,
He simply rolls and starts to flow.

These tales all swim in laughter and cheer,
A world of whimsy, where jokes adhere,
So dive right in, don't miss the fun,
For bizarre stories gather one by one.

Glimmers of the Ocean's Enchantment

The waves sparkle like shiny gems,
As sea cucumbers strike silly poses,
A light-hearted dolphin starts to sing,
While seaweed joins in, swaying in spring.

A starfish wishes for toes like yours,
While playing hide-and-seek in the floors,
As bubbles rise from a giggling clown,
Beneath the surface, they turn upside down.

The moonlight twinkles on scales so bright,
With fish throwing parties every night,
Anemones bouncing to the beat,
In this enchanted world, life can't be beat!

So let your laughter echo the tide,
In the ocean's heart, where joy resides,
For each glimmer whispers tales so rare,
Of funny moments that fill the air.

Whispers of the Ocean's Garden

The clowns in suits say, "Don't be shy,"
They juggle seaweed like a pie.
A turtle giggles, breaks the code,
A fish slips past with a big old load.

A crab wears shades, he's quite the chap,
He moonwalks sideways, can't take a nap.
A seahorse winks, says, "Look at me!"
Swaying in waves, so fancy and free.

The starfish grins, so full of cheer,
With tickles and giggles, he draws near.
He whispers secrets to the seashells,
While barnacles plot their shell-filled spells.

With bubbles and laughter, they prance around,
The ocean's our circus, the best playground.
So join the fun, don't miss the show,
In this colorful world where laughter flows!

Beneath the Coral Canopy

Beneath the branches of coral bright,
A fish in a tux does a fancy fright.
With fins a-flutter, he does a spin,
Watch out, world, here comes the fin!

A octopus mime, with tentacles sway,
Pretends to juggle all day, hooray!
The lionfish roars, but it's all in jest,
A peacock's feather takes care of the rest.

The sea cucumber says with glee,
"I'm not much of a dancer, let me be!"
The shrimp tap dance, they bring the heat,
While a clam claps along with beat.

Amongst the corals, we laugh and cheer,
With humor and joy in every sphere.
Take off your worries, join the spree,
In this watery world, we dance with glee!

Emerald Gardens of the Deep

In gardens lush, oh so emerald green,
A fish in a bowtie is quite the scene.
He twirls through reefs with such flair,
Making sea critters stop and stare.

The jellyfish floats like a goofball bright,
With chandeliers on, straying in light.
A sleepy puffer fish snorts in delight,
As a crab finds his dance moves just right.

Giant clams chuckle with pearly grins,
While shrimp form a band, and the party begins.
They tap their tiny feet on coral beds,
While everyone pops up to show off their heads.

In this garden below, the fun is supreme,
Where creatures unite and laughter's the theme.
So come join the mermaids, they'll show you how,
To swim and to frolic, and take a bow!

Dance of the Colorful Fishes

A waltz of colors, fish dart and weave,
A clownfish taught them how to believe.
They twirl and giggle, it's such a sight,
Swirling and playing, oh what a delight.

The blue tang twists with pizzazz and grace,
While the parrotfish joins in the race.
Each fin's a brushstroke, painting the tide,
In this underwater dance, we take pride.

A flounder giggles, blending in deeper,
"I'm not shy! I'm a sneakier peeper!"
The angelfish flutters, like a floating dream,
As bubbles burst forth, hissing with steam.

With laughter and joy everywhere you glance,
These colorful fishes invite you to dance.
Join the escapade, let's splash and tease,
In this oceanic waltz, let's swirl with ease!

Sanctuary of the Sea's Embrace

In a home of swirling fish,
A crab danced like a silly dish.
With a wiggly tail and clumsy feet,
He declared, 'I'm the sea's fun treat!'

The seaweed swayed in tunes of cheer,
While a dolphin flipped, oh so near.
With giggles and splashes, they played all day,
In this watery village, all worries sway.

A clownfish jokes atop a rock,
'Why did the lobster cross the block?
To get to the other tide, you see,
Where sea cucumbers sipped their tea!'

In the depths where laughter thrives,
Every creature dances, and joy arrives.
With bubbles of giggles and oceans of fun,
This sanctuary sparkles, where all are one.

Enchanted Realms Beneath the Waves.

A turtle with shades, oh what a sight,
Said, 'Surf's up, but I'm too tight!'
His friends all laughed, they couldn't stay,
While he slowly munched on kelp buffet.

The parrotfish, bold, was full of cheer,
"With bright colors, I am a pioneer!"
But he tripped on coral, fell with a splash,
Unfazed, he winked, saying, 'That was quite the crash!'

An octopus studied the latest ballet,
In eight left feet, he danced away.
Fins flapping wildly, he'd wobble and whirl,
"Who knew being graceful was such a twirl?"

As sunset hues kissed the watery scene,
The fish gathered round for the nightgate sheen.
With jokes and laughter, they splashed with glee,
In enchanted realms, where all are free.

Whispers of the Tide

A seal snorted giggles at the fishy parade,
"Can't catch me!" he shouted, causing quite the jade.
The fishes all chuckled, spinning around,
In this playful ballet, they almost fell down.

Sea stars played poker on a rock so bright,
"Four of a kind," said one, "This feels just right!"
But a crab stole the chips with a sneaky little scheme,
"Life's just a game, let's just have some cream!"

With jellyfish jiving, glowing in the dark,
They threw a party under the coral arc.
"Who invited the shrimp? They pinch like a clown!"
But all agreed, "They spice up the town!"

As waves whispered secrets old as the sea,
Every splash was filled with pure glee.
In this frolicsome world, oh so wide,
Joy rides the currents, with laughter as our guide.

Beneath the Water's Veil

A fish in a tux, twirled in delight,
Hollering, "I'm ready for my big night!"
But he slipped on a shell, made quite a clatter,
"Who knew looking sharp would end in a splatter?"

Shrimps in a line for the big show tonight,
Told each other stories with dizzying fright.
"Did you hear the one about the crab and his shell?
He thought he turned elegant, but oh, what the hell!"

Anemones blushed as the clam couple danced,
Everyone cheered, 'You've got us entranced!'
But the jellyfish sighed, saying with flair,
"Next time, please check if I'm in the air!"

With bubbles of laughter and tales to impart,
Underneath waves, they shared every part.
In a dance of the silly, the clumsy, the free,
Life beneath the veil is a comedy spree!

Symphony of the Marine Wilds

The fish all dance with glee,
In their underwater spree.
A crab plays the trombone,
While seahorses sway and moan.

A jellyfish leads the choir,
Singing songs that never tire.
But octopuses steal the show,
With eight arms putting on a glow.

The starfish just sit around,
Commenting on the sound.
They've got five points to make,
But they just sit and shake.

If you dive down for a look,
You'll find fish that write a book.
Their best seller? Under the Sea,
Full of laughs and silly glee.

Reflections in a Serpent's Pool

In a pool, a serpent floats,
Wearing sunglasses and a coat.
He claims to be a fashion king,
But all he does is wiggle and cling.

Tiny fish swim by for fun,
As he basks under the sun.
With a flip and a splash he'll say,
'Can you see my abs today?'

A turtle joins with sandwich treats,
Exchanging gossip, oh so sweet!
They talk of whales and crab-filled pies,
Under water, where the laughter flies.

But watch your toes, the snake may bite,
With a laugh, he gives a fright!
Yet all in good humor, they jest,
Swapping stories, they're truly blessed.

The Depths of Color's Embrace

Down where colors twist and churn,
There's a clownfish with much to learn.
He darts and dives with all his flair,
But still can't figure out his hair.

Anemones poke and tease him bright,
"Style your fins with all your might!"
"Oh hush," he replies in a whine,
"I'm fabulous under this sunshine!"

A parrotfish turns into a brush,
Painting corals with a happy rush.
Each stroke is a giggle, a splash of fun,
An underwater party has just begun!

With bubbles of laughter, they create,
A masterpiece that can't wait.
And while colors blend and mix,
They find humor in their tricks.

Lost Treasures of the Seabed

Down below, where pirates roam,
A treasure chest became a home.
Fish peek in, they look quite sly,
"What's in there?" They dream and sigh.

A mermaid claims it holds a shoe,
With rhinestones that somehow grew.
"Oh darling," says a cheeky flounder,
"Your tales are less than sounding wonder!"

"Let's dive deeper, let's find more!"
A group of friends swims to explore.
They search for gold and shiny rings,
But find a sock and broken strings!

With laughter bubbling from each fish,
They trade their finds with a swish and swish.
And though treasures may be in their heads,
It's fun to uncover what lies in their beds.

Tides of Vibrant Life

In the ocean's dress, a bright parade,
Fish in bow ties, not afraid.
Crabs do the tango on the sand,
While seahorses ride the latest trend.

Oysters gossip with shells a-clack,
Starfish find their way to the snack.
Anemones wave like they own the show,
With clownfish giggling all in a row.

Octopuses juggling with style so grand,
Each tentacle moves, perfectly planned.
A turtle winks, oh what a sight!
Streaming past, they dance in delight.

Every wave brings a quirky twist,
In this watery world, you can't resist.
Life is a splash in a sea so vast,
With laughs and marbles, we have a blast.

In the Heart of the Coral Garden

Snapper in shades, looking so cool,
While parrotfish paint, acting the fool.
A group of pufferfish full of jest,
Sucking it up, they float with zest.

Clownfish are clowns, giving a wink,
In bubble homes, they totally sync.
An octopus hides with a shy little wave,
Trying so hard to be just brave.

The shrimp dance a line like they've won the prize,
With costumes made from the ocean's disguise.
With a laugh and a whirl, they put on a show,
In vibrant hues that make the sea glow.

Jellyfish float like balloons on a string,
While sea turtles groove to the tunes they bring.
All in this garden where chuckles reside,
Life is a circus, come enjoy the ride!

Sunlit Canopies Below

In a sunbeam grove, the gobies play,
Singing fish tales throughout the day.
A lionfish struts with a feathered flair,
While shrimps do the cha-cha without a care.

Under the waves where the laughter blooms,
Urchins throw parties in colorful rooms.
Clams crack jokes as they open wide,
While tunas laugh at their speedy glide.

Wrasse hold court, giving their best jest,
With chortles and chuckles, they pass the test.
As currents swirl, all creatures unite,
In this canvas below, everything feels right.

So come take a dip in this playful spree,
Where every corner holds a mystery.
Bubbles of laughter float up to the sky,
In the sunlit depths, let your worries fly!

The Symphony of Sea Creatures

In the undersea band, each plays a tune,
With trumpetfish blowing under the moon.
A grouper on drums keeps the beat just right,
While seaweed sways in the shimmering light.

The dolphins add vocals, oh what a sound,
Echoing joy all around and around.
With tails that swish and fins that flap,
They put on a show, no one needs a map.

Tropical fish sing in a colorful line,
Casting their scales, oh so divine.
In this orchestra of joy, tune in please,
As laughter and music ride every breeze.

The ocean's a symphony, bright and absurd,
With sea creatures jamming in a world unheard.
So join in the fun, let your spirit soar,
In the serenade where life is never a bore!

The Calling of Distant Shores

There once was a crab with a funny hat,
He danced on the sand, oh, imagine that!
A seagull laughed, then took a dive,
While fish swam by, feeling alive.

The wave said, "Splash! Come join the fun!"
"But I'm busy sunbathing!" said the stubborn one.
With each little wave, he rolled and tumbled,
The crab just giggled as he stumbled.

From shells and flippers, tunes did play,
As dolphins jumped in a jazzy ballet.
The crab took a bow, under the sun's glare,
Waving his claws like he just didn't care!

So if you wander to this sandy retreat,
Look for that crab with shuffling feet.
Join in the chaos, the laughter will soar,
And the calling of distant shores will be more!

Shells and Stars - A Connection

A clam claimed a star, put it on his shell,
He said, "I'll be famous, and you can tell!"
A hermit crab chuckled, rolling his eyes,
"That's not how fame works! Have you heard the wise?"

As the tide rolled in, shells danced about,
A conch shell trumpeted—a joyful shout!
The stars in the sky blinked in surprise,
"Why are there so many, is this a disguise?"

The anemone giggled, waving its arms,
"They're just jealous of our underwater charms!"
Even the seaweed swayed with glee,
Creating a party on the deep blue spree.

With laughter and bubbles, they swirled around,
In this ocean fiesta, silliness found.
So grab your best shell, come join the fun,
With shells and stars, we'll shine like the sun!

A Whirlwind of Tidal Colors

In the ocean's backyard, a rainbow swirled,
Fish wore colors, bright and twirled.
A clownfish laughed, said, "Look at me!"
"I'm the star of this watery jamboree!"

As squids inked stories, a colorful show,
Octopuses danced—what a wild glow!
An urchin unrolled its spiky crown,
"This party's going to take us all down!"

The seahorses swayed in a two-step jig,
While wrasses giggled, they felt quite big.
And turtles slowly joined, with their laid-back style,
Creating a snappy, underwater smile.

With splashes and giggles, the fun did ignite,
In a whirlwind of hues, they danced through the night.
A tapestry woven with joy and delight,
In the ocean's colors, oh, what a sight!

Harmony in the Ocean's Embrace

A jellyfish floated with grace so rare,
Bouncing along like it didn't have a care.
A grouper swam by, saying, "What's up?"
"Just dancing like jelly, what about you, pup?"

"Let's harmonize," the pufferfish said,
With a puff and a giggle—it bounced right ahead.
The sea cucumbers nodded, joining the beat,
Grooving together, they felt so sweet!

The tides whispered jokes, the bubbles joined in,
Creating a symphony of laughter and spin.
With each little wave, more critters swayed,
In this funny ballet, all worries decayed.

So come take a plunge, where the fun never ceases,
In harmony's arms, the spirit releases.
The ocean's embrace is a joyful affair,
Where laughter and giggles float freely in air!

Visions in Coral Phantasmagoria

Underwater tea parties, fish wear a hat,
Starfish flipping pancakes, how about that?
Octopus plays chess with a sly little grin,
Whales gossip about the latest fin spin.

Jellyfish float in gowns, they're so chic,
Clownfish telling jokes, making us squeak.
Sea turtles are judges in this strange game,
And every new splash is a candid fame.

Shrimps in tuxedos, they serve shrimp cocktails,
While dolphins perform acrobatics and tales.
Anemones dance as they wave and sway,
In this marine circus, we laugh all day.

The ocean is batty, with humor to spare,
Where sea cucumbers look debonair.
With bubbles and giggles, the tides shall crest,
In this underwater realm, we find laughter's best.

The Dance of Color and Light

A clownfish in slippers just took to the floor,
With seahorses twirling, who could ask for more?
Corals are disco balls, glowing so bright,
As fish spin around, what a curious sight!

A crab doing the cha-cha, all claws in the air,
While eels serenade from their underwater lair.
Stingrays glide smoothly, with hustles and spins,
Even the barnacles clap with their skins.

Tropical colors paint a vibrant affair,
As a flounder shows off with his crazy flair.
The rhythm of currents, it beckons our toes,
In this jovial waltz where the sea laughter flows.

With bubbles and swirls, the ocean does sway,
Join the giggles, dance the day away!
In the depths of the waves, let our spirits take flight,
For joy is abundant in this shimmering light.

An Ocean's Palette

Colors colliding like a paint-splattered dream,
Fish in bright hues burst out in a gleam.
With reds like a chili and blues that entice,
Even sea urchins are feeling precise.

Starfish do pirouettes on rocks oh so bright,
While seaweed sways gently, catching the light.
Coral formations, like castles so grand,
Whisper secrets to shells on the soft sand.

A tangy green sea cucumber leans in for cheer,
'The ocean's our canvas, let laughter steer!'
Pufferfish bobbing, look, isn't it weird?
While clownfish are giggling, they're ever so teared.

Joy drips like paint, coloring all in sight,
With every new wave, the hues feel just right.
In this artful ocean, let humor be free,
As nature's great palette paints fun near the sea.

Unveiling Nature's Sculptures

Oh, the sculptures of nature, made from pure brine,
With crabs that are sculptors, crafting designs.
Anemones sway like they're painted by hand,
And sea sponges whisper, 'Isn't this grand?'

Clownfish frolic like they own a fine muse,
While turtles pose perfectly, striking their views.
Corals look majestic, as they bloom and unfold,
A gallery of wonders, both lively and bold.

The sculptors of water, make art every day,
Dolphins diving, creating bright ballet.
Sea fans waving their brushes in delight,
As laughter and art mingle deep in the night.

In this gallery below, the fun never ends,
For nature's great magic, it surely transcends.
With giggles and whimsy, we're drawn to the show,
As sculptures of laughter make the ocean glow.

Secrets of the Shimmering Depths

The crab wore shoes that were too tight,
He shuffled sideways, what a sight!
The clownfish laughed, with cheeks so round,
As bubbles burst and danced around.

An octopus wore an old top hat,
Trying to charm a curious cat.
With eight swift arms he waved and spun,
While starfish giggled, oh what fun!

A turtle told tales of days gone by,
As eels swayed gently, oh my, oh my!
With every tale, the laughter grew,
As seaweed danced, a vibrant crew.

In the depths, where laughter glows,
Underwater jokes, as everyone knows,
The secrets shared by fins and tails,
Bring giggles that ride the watery trails.

Dances of the Colorful Fishes

The fishes gathered for a grand parade,
In rainbow colors, brightly displayed.
They twirled and spun in a silly way,
Each trying to outshine the next ballet.

The pufferfish puffed, but got stuck tight,
He rolled on the sand, oh what a sight!
With every bounce, he giggled so loud,
While sea cucumbers formed a proud crowd.

A parrotfish whistled a merry tune,
As seahorses danced under the moon.
Their fins flapped fast, a comical sight,
In the shimmering glow of the ocean light.

With bubbles rising, laughter did grow,
As turtles joined in the waltz, oh no!
They clumsily spun and tripped on their feet,
Creating a rhythm that was hard to beat.

The Echoes of Aquatic Dreams

In the depths, where echoes swirl,
A fish took a dive with a daring twirl.
He called to the clams, all huddled tight,
"Hey, let's jam under the pale moonlight!"

A dolphin came in, with a splash and a grin,
"Is this the party? Let the fun begin!"
With clicks and whistles, they made quite a sound,
As the octopus danced, spinning round and round.

The jellyfish glowed, like lanterns bright,
Floating along with pure delight.
But one little shrimp, with a joke to share,
Said, "Keep your tentacles out of my hair!"

The laughter bubbled, as seaweed shook,
While fish found verses in every nook.
With echoes of joy filling the sea,
These aquatic dreams are so funny and free!

Lullaby of the Ocean Floor

At the bottom where the sand is soft,
The sea slugs sang, in voices aloft.
Their lullabies floated like gentle waves,
As sleepy critters sought cozy caves.

The hermit crab found a home quite snug,
In an old shoe—now that's a hug!
He settled in, with a yawn so deep,
As fish swirled 'round, in a drowsy heap.

The sea stars twinkled in slumber's embrace,
While sleepy flounders found their space.
With a wink and a nudge, they dreamt a tale,
Of jellybean castles that never would pale.

With each sleepy sound, the ocean sighed,
In this underwater world, they joyfully abide.
As laughter faded into dreams so sweet,
A lullaby drifted, making life complete.

Chronicles of the Fishmonger's Yarns

In waters deep, a fish told a joke,
A squid laughed hard, it nearly choked.
The crab joined in with a pinch of flair,
'This sea's a circus, so pull up a chair!'

A jellyfish danced, all swirls and spins,
While starfish grinned with mischievous grins.
The octopus served drinks with his eight arms,
'Ladies and gents, I bring you charms!'

Fish frantically flipped for the grand buffet,
'Watch out for the catch, and don't swim away!'
The dolphin chuckled, diving past fast,
'In this underwater ball, we have a blast!'

And so they laughed in their watery room,
Creating mischief amidst the gloom.
With bubbles of giggles, they built a scene,
A comedic splash, where all could glean.

Fall of the Silent Ocean Light

A lobster wearing sunglasses, oh so proud,
Chasing jellybeans, he feels quite loud.
The sea cucumbers roll on the floor,
'Why do we flop? We were made to explore!'

A fish with a hat asked, 'What's the deal?'
The clam replied, 'We just keep it real!'
While krill threw a party, complete with cake,
They danced in the waves, for goodness' sake!

A turtle with dreams of grand ballet,
Tried spinning and twisting in a wild way.
The gulls above watched, shaking their heads,
'Look at those fish; they're crazier than threads!'

And as the currents swayed and spun,
The ocean giggled, calling it fun.
In silent depths, laughter rang out bright,
A playful scene under the moonlight.

The Sea's Hidden Canvas

In depths of blue, where colors collide,
A clownfish painted portraits with pride.
With coral brushes, they splashed and swung,
'What's next?' asked the eel, as he brightly sung.

A parrotfish shouted, 'Let's add some cheer!'
Swirling pebbles, it spread the good cheer.
The sea stars twinkled, flinging in hues,
A masterpiece seen by the fishes and crews.

With laughter and bubbles, they dashed all about,
'Oh, look at our art! There's no room for doubt!'
A seahorse giggled with a creative turn,
'Art is best made with a splash and a churn!'

Together they danced, a colorful sight,
With a stroke of fun, they lit up the night.
The ocean's canvas, a vibrant parade,
A world of humor, joy never delayed.

Enchanted Depths and Ancient Mysteries

In enchanted depths, where secrets hide,
A fishy detective with confidence tried.
'What's that over there? A treasure so sweet!'
'Oh no,' said a crab, 'Just my lunch on repeat!'

Amidst ancient tales and beautiful sights,
The seaweed swayed while it giggled at nights.
'What's lost in the sea? A shoe or a sock?'
The pufferfish pondered, all puffed like a rock.

They found a lost sock and gave it a whirl,
'This sea's a vast closet!' said one little pearl.
A dolphin flipped high, shouting, 'Look, I found gold!'
'That's just a bottle cap!' laughed the school, uncontrolled.

With bubbles of laughter, they carried on light,
In depths where the odd and the funny unite.
Through ancient whispers and whimsical times,
The ocean sang out, all in silly rhymes.

Coral Castles and Ocean Dreams

In castles made of coral bright,
The fish throw parties every night.
They dance on waves, a silly scene,
Wearing shells and seaweed, quite the routine.

A crab DJ spins, oh what a sight,
While starfish twirl under moonlight.
An octopus juggles pearls galore,
While sea turtles shout, "We want more!"

Clams sing opera, oh so bold,
Their voices echo, never old.
A seahorse leads the conga line,
With all the critters feeling fine.

So dive on in, don't miss the fun,
Join the party, everyone!
For beneath the waves, laughter rings,
In this realm where joy is king.

Mysteries of the Blue Abyss

In the depths, a mystery swirls,
With dancing eels and shiny pearls.
A fish wears glasses, oh what a sight,
Claiming it's the smartest of the night.

A whale gets lost in a game of tag,
While jellyfish do their own brag.
They float like balloons, with grace and flair,
In a world where sea creatures dare.

A deep-sea squid tries to play chess,
But loses to a crab in a total mess.
They laugh and laugh, such silly fun,
In the depths of a world where the sun can't run.

So come take a peek, bring your cheer,
Discover the follies that swim near.
For under the waves, where the giggles flow,
Lies a realm of hilarity you must know!

Odes to the Ocean Floor

Upon the ocean floor so grand,
Live creatures with a rock band.
A clam strums softly on his shell,
While sea anemones sway and yell.

A pufferfish tries to sing a tune,
But pops himself—oh, what a ruin!
The sea cucumbers laugh, oh dear,
While a dolphin squeals, "Best show of the year!"

The seaweed flows like a dancer mild,
With crabs doing the shuffle, quite wild!
Hilarious moments fill the tide,
As laughter spreads, nothing to hide.

So venture down where the fun is bright,
Join the chorus of delights alight.
For on the ocean floor, life's a dream,
With giggles that ripple like a sparkling stream!

Beneath the Surface: A Hidden Realm

Beneath the waves, a secret space,
Where sea creatures laugh and race.
A clownfish jokes, "I'm no real clown,
Just here to turn your frown upside down!"

The sea turtles wear disco hats,
And cha-cha with the chatting gnats.
Octopus doubles as a face painter,
Creating looks that could be a gainer!

A school of fish holds a talent show,
With mesmerizing dances, go fish, go!
But watch out, here comes a sneaky shark,
Who just wants to join in on the spark.

So drift along, don't you be shy,
Where laughter bubbles and spirits fly.
For beneath the surface, joy runs free,
In this happy place, come laugh with me!

Tidal Dreams and Driftwood Tales

Waves roll in with a giggle,
Seaweed dances, oh so wiggle.
Starfish look like they're on break,
Crabs gossip, oh what a fake!

Clams are hiding pearls so grand,
Wish they'd share; it's not in hand.
Jellyfish float in silly ways,
Like they're lost in dizzy bays.

Seagulls laugh at the clown fish,
They just wanted a flying dish.
Sandcastles fall, then they cheer,
Oops! Who built that? Not me, dear!

Seashells tell their stories bright,
Of chasing waves till they get light.
In this world, laughter holds sway,
Every tide brings a new play!

Where the Rays Whisper

In the depths, the rays convene,
Sharing giggles, what a scene!
They tickle fish with their soft wings,
Making bubbles, oh how it stings!

Their laughter echoes through the sea,
As fish join in, wild and free.
A dolphin leaps with a loud snort,
Turning shallow waters to sport!

As crabs hide under rocks so sly,
Watching the fun with a sharp eye.
Who knew the ocean's full of jest?
Every wave, a playful quest!

When twilight calls the stars to glow,
The dolphins hold a night-time show.
With every splash, a story flows,
In these waters where laughter grows!

Phantom Shadows in Water

In the blue, shadows flit about,
Making fish scream and shout.
With silly masks, they prank and play,
Who has the best ghostly sway?

Octopuses twist into a knot,
A game of tag is what they've got.
But tangled up, they've lost the score,
Oh dear, chaos swims ashore!

Eels slip by with a playful grin,
Trying hard to reel us in.
Behind the rocks, a surprise awaits,
A sassy shrimp with funny traits!

The day turns dark, but joy remains,
In underwater joke domains.
So fear not the shadows that creep,
For laughter's the treasure we keep!

Portraits of the Submerged

In vibrant hues, art takes a dive,
Each fish flaunts its look, alive!
A parrotfish poses with flair,
"Check my colors, see if you dare!"

Clownfish prance in their best threads,
"They can't catch us!" is what one said.
The sea anemone grins so wide,
"I'm the star, come watch my ride!"

Starfish strike a pose, so bold,
In the spotlight, they feel gold.
Every scale sparkles with glee,
A gallery under the sea!

As the tide shifts, they change their tune,
Painting smiles beneath the moon.
With each splash, they add to their art,
In this world, laughter fills the heart!

Chronicles of the Fathomless

In depths of blue, where fish swim free,
A starfish ponders, in deep irony.
Why walk on legs, when I can just stick?
Life's a funny dance, not a calculus trick.

A crab in a tux, with snappy attire,
Dances with shrimp, set their hearts on fire.
"Two left feet?" they chuckle, shaking with glee,
Underwater jamboree, who needs a TV?

A turtle named Tim, got a shell full of zest,
Calls over the dolphins for a weekend fest.
"Last one to the reef is a guppy!" they cheer,
While Tim just floats, sipping kelp-flavored beer.

So join this parade in the watery realm,
Where giggles and bubbles take up the helm.
With laughter resounding and spirits so bright,
Even the seaweed sways, full of delight.

Life in a Fractured Paradise

In a place where clams gossip over the tide,
A lobster grumbles, 'Can't find my side!'.
He checks his mirrors, sleek and so fine,
But crabs keep pinching—it's truly divine.

An octopus juggling, with eight arms a-whirl,
Mistakes a fish for his favorite pearl.
"Oh dear!" he gasps, "Did I grab your fin?"
A seafood circus—let the fun begin!

The sea cucumbers dance, if you could call it that,
Reminiscing glory of days when they sat.
"Let's roll with the tide!" they cheerfully murmur,
Finding joy in the silt as they wiggle and squirmer.

In this offbeat world, laughter is the way,
Where pufferfish pop in a humorous display.
From rays that flutter to seahorses twirl,
Life's a strange comedy in this loose-limbed whirl.

The Blush of Sea Anemones

Beneath the waves dwell, the shy and the bold,
Where anemones blush, their secrets unfold.
With clownfish buzzing—what a ragtag crew,
They joke 'bout the ocean, and all it can do.

"Here's a tale!" said one with stripes black and white,
"I once met a whale, who thought he could kite."
With laughter erupting, from the nooks they hide,
They hug their soft arms, feel their joy collide.

The eels tell stories of shocking pursuits,
While pirate fish swashbuckle in glittery suits.
"What's treasure?" they jest, "Is it pearls or a seat?
Or just good old company? Now that's quite the feat!"

With bubbles of giggles, they spin and they sway,
In this watery kingdom, where fun rules the day.
The blush of the garden, it sparkles and gleams,
Where friendship runs deep, and humor redeems.

Echoes of the Undercurrent

In the undercurrent whispers, fish make their bets,
A grouper starts pondering—what's with all the nets?
"Caught a great meal," he brags to his peers,
While a sardine snickers, "I'll swim off my tears!"

The flounder's a master of hide-and-seek,
But rays just glide by with a confident cheek.
"Catch me if you can!" the fish giggle and play,
As dolphins dive low and scream out hooray!

A sea urchin moans, with its spines all akimbo,
"Who invited the squid? All the ink—it's a bimbo!"
They all erupt laughing, in this salty café,
Where humor's the spice on a bright ocean day.

With echoes of laughter, the tide ebbs and flows,
These tales of the depths spark joy as it goes.
Through quirks and their laughter, a melody found,
In the heart of the ocean, where joy does abound.

Serendipity in the Reef's Embrace

A fish in a bowtie, what a sight,
It dances around, full of delight.
Clams throw a party, but crustaceans scowl,
Crabs in tuxedos trying to howl.

Octopus juggling, a real head-scratcher,
While seaweed sways to a tune much ratcher.
Starfish gossiping about the tide,
As dolphins swoop in for a wild ride.

The anemones giggle, tickled by waves,
Silly little shrimp pretending to rave.
Lionfish strut like they're on a show,
While eels hide away, feeling quite low.

What a scene beneath sparkling blue,
Where even a clam can be seen in a shoe.
So, join in the fun, take a peek underneath,
In this world of wonders, all that's beneath.

Mosaic of the Ocean's Heart

A turtle in sunglasses is making a splash,
As fish in a school form a glittery stash.
The rocks are adorned with a jellyfish crown,
While seahorses laugh at the wave-pounding clown.

Nemo's lost again, can't find his way,
But finds a new friend who loves to play.
They slide down the kelp with giggles and squeals,
While crabs in the background flash smiles with their heels.

The grouper tells stories, tall tales all around,
About a big shark who never was found.
The snails roll their eyes, they're quite in the know,
Shaking their shells in a rhythm they flow.

With each curious glance at the colorful scene,
Life down below is quite silly and keen.
The currents hum a tune that's bright,
In this underwater world, everything's light.

The Serenity of Submerged Flora

Corals are blooming, a colorful spree,
While seaweed's doing the twist—oh, can't you see?
A parrotfish giggles at his reflection,
Complaining about his bad shell selection.

Hydrozoans whisper secrets to silt,
As barnacles gather for a sushi quilt.
Sponges throw shade while munching on glee,
Orange peel mantas claim 'Join us for tea!'

The kelp's throwing parties, with fronds all aglow,
While surf clams perform in a rhythmic flow.
Anemones laugh, waving arms like a band,
As they invite the fish to join hand in hand.

Sunlight sparkles, it wiggles and sways,
In this vibrant realm where the odd always plays.
So grab your fins, take a dip and swirl,
In the dance of life, all around it will twirl.

Guardians of the Aquatic Symphony

A lobster's conducting, what a surprise,
With shells all around, for an orchestra rise.
Sea turtles cheer with a slow, graceful motion,
As clownfish join in with a giggling notion.

Grouper strums deep like a bass in a ball,
While puffers pucker up, making the call.
The cliques are all dancing, all thrumming with joy,
As eels get tangled—what a goofy ploy!

The shells chime like bells, ringing out clear,
While shrimp do their shimmy, with little to fear.
The angelfish swirl, their colors a rush,
Spreading laughter around in an ocean-wide hush.

A playful current sweeps laughter along,
As crabs march in time to the underwater song.
So join in the fun, don't miss the sweet beat,
In this raucous ensemble, life's just a treat!

www.ingramcontent.com/pod-product-compliance
Lightning Source LLC
Chambersburg PA
CBHW072135070526
44585CB00016B/1687